PRAY: IS GOD LISTENING

RICHARD W. DE HAAN

with David C. Egner

Zondervan Publishing House
Grand Rapids, Michigan

PRAY: GOD IS LISTENING

Daybreak Books are published by the Zondervan Publishing House
1415 Lake Drive, S.E., Grand Rapids, Michigan 49506

Library of Congress Cataloging-in-Publication Data

DeHaan, Richard W.
Pray, God is listening.
"Daybreak Books."
1. Prayer. I. Egner, David C. II. Title.
BV210.2.D42 1989 248.3'2 88-20537
ISBN 0-310-23541-3

Edited by Nia Jones

Printed in the United States of America

90 91 92 93 94 95 / ML / 10

Contents

1

Questions About Prayer

WHAT A WONDERFUL privilege—we can actually talk with God! Think of it! The heavenly Father has told us to come to Him with our needs, our praise, and our most heartfelt desires. Yes, we can pray to God. He is listening!

Yet isn't it strange that though we have God's gracious invitation to come boldly to the throne of grace, so few of us do? Isn't it sad that even though we've been commanded to pray, very few of us actually spend time with the Lord?

What's wrong? Why do we neglect one of the most blessed provisions God has given us? How can Christians go for days and even months without really engaging in genuine and fervent prayer?

With some, I'm sure it's simply a matter of spiritual lethargy—of backsliding. With others, the failure to pray is caused by the pressures of life, such as their job or their family responsibilities. But that's just when they need prayer the most. Still others neglect it because of ignorance about the nature of prayer and what God expects of us.

I firmly believe that every Christian should understand what the Bible teaches about prayer. A successful, effective prayer life is built on a solid scriptural foundation. That's why we are discussing this important subject.

I would like to begin by answering these five basic questions about prayer:

1. Who can pray?
2. Why do we pray?
3. Where do we pray?
4. When do we pray?
5. How should we pray?

WHO CAN PRAY?

Some people say that prayer is an avenue to God that is open to all people, whether they are saved or unsaved, wicked or righteous. Others claim that God hears only the prayers of believers in Jesus Christ. Now, who is right?

I believe that only those people who know the Lord through faith in His Son, the Lord Jesus Christ, and who are walking in fellowship with Him, can have the confidence that their prayers are accepted by the Father in heaven. The Bible tells us:

> For the eyes of the Lord are on the righteous, and His ears are open to their prayers; but the face of the LORD is against those who do evil (1 Peter 3:12).

The apostle Peter said that God hears the prayers of the righteous. But what about the ungodly? Does God respect their prayers? Are His ears open to their cries? The answer is given in the last part of the verse. Although Peter assured the righteous that God honors their prayers, he went on to say, ". . . but the face of the Lord is *against* those who do evil."

Only those who have believed in Christ and are walking in fellowship with Him have the exclusive right to come to the Lord with confidence that their prayers are heard. We must be careful, however, not to say that God never responds to the cries of sinners. He certainly has the right to grant the requests of anyone—even someone unsaved—according to His own sovereign will and righteous purposes. And, of course, He always accepts the "sinner's prayer." That's the prayer for salvation. The

Bible says, "For whoever calls upon the name of the Lord shall be saved" (Rom. 10:13).

He is God. He sees, hears, and knows everything going on in the world. He is aware whenever anyone—righteous or unrighteous—prays. But only believers have the assurance that when they come to the Father, He will answer their prayers with loving and special consideration.

WHY DO WE PRAY?

Why has God told us to pray? First of all, it is the way for us to enjoy fellowship and communion with Him. In a quiet place away from the hustle and bustle of the world, we sense His presence and rejoice in the awareness of His nearness.

Edward Keith tells us, "Prayer is exhaling the spirit of man and inhaling the Spirit of God." Through prayer our weakness is exchanged for God's power.

Second, we pray to ask the Lord for His help in time of need. The author of Hebrews wrote:

> Let us therefore come boldly to the throne of grace, that we may obtain mercy and find grace to help in time of need (Heb. 4:16).

We don't know or understand everything about prayer. But this much is certain: We can enter God's presence asking for the gracious bestowal of good gifts from God's hand. We can therefore come to Him expressing our needs.

Here's the third and most important reason to pray: It is God's will. The apostle Paul entreated:

> Therefore I desire that the men pray everywhere, lifting up holy hands, without wrath and doubting (1 Tim. 2:8).

And Jesus Himself said, ". . . men always ought to pray and not lose heart" (Luke 18:1). Yes, it is God's will that we pray. It pleases Him when we come to the throne of grace, acknowledging our dependence on Him, asking what we need of Him, and demonstrating our faith in Him. And prayer has power! Tennyson said, "More things are wrought by prayer than this world dreams of."

WHERE DO WE PRAY?

Who is able to tell us where we can pray? Can we pray only in church? Or only in so-called sacred places? Or daily at some altar? The answer is that we can pray *everywhere*! We are to pray in the church, of course, but God wants us to come to Him wherever we might be.

Our physical surroundings should never restrict us or discourage us from praying. Jonah prayed from the belly of a fish. Paul prayed in prison. Daniel prayed before an open window in his own room. Hannah, the mother of Samuel, poured out her heart to the Lord in the tabernacle. Jesus prayed in a garden. And after the resurrection, the followers of Christ were found praying in an upper room in the city of Jerusalem. Wherever we are, we can commune with our heavenly Father in prayer. At any time, in any place, we have the privilege and freedom of talking to God.

True, some places are set aside especially for prayer and worship. They provide a quiet, conducive atmosphere for united prayer with fellow believers. But foolish is the person who waits to open his heart to God until he is in a so-called place of prayer. Remember, we can pray wherever we are, whenever a need arises, and as the Spirit directs us.

WHEN DO WE PRAY?

Should people pray only in response to the ringing of a bell or a call from a minaret five times a day? Is it only a mealtime and bedtime exercise? Should we pray only when we are led by a minister? Of course not. We are to pray anywhere and anytime; in fact, *all the time*. The Bible says, "Pray without ceasing" (1 Thess. 5:17).

Obviously, we can't run around with our eyes closed all the time engaged in formal prayer, or even breathing silent prayers. We have work to do. Obligations must be met. And we must leave time for rest and relaxation.

What then did Paul mean when he said, "Pray without ceasing"? Let me present two possible explanations. He might have meant that we should always be in close fellowship with God and living with such an awareness of His presence that prayer comes as naturally as breathing itself. Then, when a need arises, when a problem confronts us, or when we're reminded of a friend in distress, we can breathe a prayer to God right on the spot. Whenever we think of God's goodness, His love for us, and His grace, we can offer our thanks. We can express our praise to the Lord as naturally as we can talk to our closest friend.

Praying without ceasing could also mean that there should be no break in our pattern of prayer. In other words, there should never be any period in our lives that is characterized by prayerlessness. We should always be in the attitude of prayer.

Regular, specified times for prayer are of great value. The habit of the prophet Daniel is a good example.

> Now when Daniel knew that the writing was signed, he went home. And in his upper room, with his windows open toward Jerusalem, he knelt down on his knees three times that day, and prayed and gave thanks before his God, as was his custom since early days (Daniel 6:10).

And David the psalmist wrote:

> Evening and morning and at noon I will pray, and cry aloud, and He shall hear my voice (Ps. 55:17).

We should have regular quiet times when we are alone with God and isolated from all distractions. We should spend time with Him in communion, confession, petition, and intercession. But it is also true that wherever we are, and whatever we may be doing, we can talk with God as friend to friend.

HOW SHOULD WE PRAY?

Is there any special way that Christians should come to the Lord in prayer? Are we to assume a special posture? Are there any prerequisites?

First, we must pray in faith. The author of the Epistle to the Hebrews wrote:

> But without faith it is impossible to please Him, for he who comes to God must believe that He is, and that He is a rewarder of those who diligently seek Him (Heb. 11:6).

If you don't believe that God exists, it's ridiculous to pray. And it's wasted effort if you are not convinced that He has the power to answer your prayers. So you must exercise faith. You must believe when you pray. The poet wrote:

> Faith, mighty faith, the promise sees
> And looks to God alone;
> Laughs at impossibilities
> And cries, "It shall be done!"

As we offer God our petitions, our worship, and our intercession, we ought to believe that His goodness, His greatness, and His glory will work together to give us what is right and best for us.

Second, we must pray to God with clean hands and a pure heart. The psalmist said, "If I regard iniquity in my heart, the Lord will not hear" (Ps. 66:18). My friend, we cannot come to the Lord of glory in waywardness, rebellion, or open sin and expect our petitions to be answered.

Third, we must pray in submission to God's will. The idea that prayer is wresting some favor from the hand of a reluctant God is erroneous. It is not a matter of our will against His. Rather, we should be submissive to God's plan and be ready to accept whatever He sends.

Remember, God is omniscient. His answers are always right; they are always the best. The Lord Himself, when praying to the Father, said, "Nevertheless not My will, but Yours, be done" (Luke 22:42). God honors those who acknowledge Him in all their ways, and who trustingly leave the answers to Him.

Fourth, we must come to the Lord with reverence. In recent days the practice of prayer has undergone some drastic changes. We now have sentence prayers, silent prayers, conversational prayers, and dial-a-prayers. Now, I'm not against those things. In fact, I'm for them and I encourage them. But in our endeavors to get more people to pray, we must remember God's holiness and the sanctity of His presence. We must never be flippant or unmindful of the One we are talking to.

When we pray, we are communicating with God, the one Supreme Being, the Lord of heaven and earth. The psalmist wrote, "Holy and awesome is His name" (Ps. 111:9). We must give Him honor. To be irreverent is to soil the red carpet of God's gracious invitation to pray.

SELF-STUDY

1. How would you evaluate your feelings about your personal prayer life?

    _____ Satisfied with it.
    _____ Needs some improvement.
    _____ Not satisfied with it.

2. List three reasons why we should pray.

    a.
    b.
    c.

3. After carefully reading this chapter, mark the following statements *True* or *False*:

    _____ (a) Prayers from the sanctuary are more effective than from other places.
    _____ (b) We should be ready to pray at any time.
    _____ (c) If we don't kneel when we pray, God won't hear us.
    _____ (d) Prayer is forcing God to do what we want.

4. What four suggestions were given about how to pray?

    a.
    b.
    c.
    d.

Challenge Question: How long has it been since one of your prayers lasted more than 2 or 3 minutes?

2

Five Elements of Prayer

HAVE YOU EVER stopped to think about all the prayers God hears every day? Have you ever tried to imagine all the things people talk about and ask for in prayer? I'm sure it would be interesting to "wiretap" the prayer line to heaven and listen in on the great, unending volume of prayer that is offered up to God. Some people are praising and thanking Him. Others are crying for relief from pain. Some are asking the Lord to unleash His vengeance against an enemy. Others are coaching God on how to handle a difficult situation. Yes, what a variety of petitions we would hear if we could only place a "wiretap" on the prayer line to heaven.

As interesting as that might be, however, it would also be disappointing. We would quickly learn how far short most people fall, even believers, from engaging in one of man's greatest privileges in the way God intended. In most cases, we would find that prayer is simply a "gimme-gimme" sort of thing. We would discover that many people pray only when they want something, and others talk to God only when they are afraid. Some use prayer to impress people with their piety. They are always eager to pray in public, but they hardly ever come to God in private.

The majority of God's people, it seems, overlook the real purpose and function of prayer. They fail to reach the ideal this blessed spiritual exercise is intended to accomplish in the life of every believer. I'm sure that God in heaven must be disappointed by what He hears—and what He does not hear.

I believe many Christians today need to place a proper emphasis on what they say when they pray. It's not enough simply to make contact with God. There must be content—that which gives our prayers substance and power. I'd like you to think with me in this chapter about the five basic elements of prayer: worship, thanksgiving, confession, petition, and intercession. As we study together, my heart's desire is that you will carefully evaluate what you say when you talk to God. Then, my hope is that you will do what you should to make your prayer life everything God wants it to be.

WORSHIP

Jesus indicated the importance of worship in His great treatise on prayer when He said:

> When you pray, say: Our Father in heaven, hallowed be Your name. Your kingdom come. Your will be done on earth as it is in heaven. Give us day by day our daily bread. And forgive us our sins, for we also forgive everyone who is indebted to us. And do not lead us into temptation, but deliver us from the evil one (Luke 11:2–4).

Please notice the opening words of Jesus' model prayer: "Our Father in heaven, hallowed be Your name." That involves worship. To hallow God's name is to honor it above all other names. When you do that with sincerity, you are not only worshiping and praising God for what He has done, but even more important, for what and who He is. You will praise Him for His power, wisdom, glory, holiness, righteousness, justice, mercy, and longsuffering.

A good way to begin your prayers is with an outpouring of adoration and love for God. You might want to include some of the great praise passages of the Scriptures in your prayer. For example, you could join the angels in saying:

> Amen! Blessing and glory and wisdom and thanksgiving and honor and power and might be to our God forever and ever. Amen (Rev. 7:12).

Even though Jesus used the expression "Hallowed be Your name" in His model prayer, I strongly suggest that you avoid the pitfall of merely repeating those exact words. Don't let them become only a mechanical expression. Instead, as you think about His greatness and goodness, use language of your own choice to offer Him your worship and praise.

When you go to the Father in prayer, remember that you are in His divine presence. Offer the God of all creation the worship He truly deserves. Reflect on His greatness and acknowledge the perfection that belongs to Him alone. As you do, your spirit will be uplifted, and your sense of God's presence will increase. And the Lord Himself will receive your adoration.

THANKSGIVING

The second essential element of prayer is thanksgiving.

> Therefore I exhort first of all that supplications, prayers, intercessions, and giving of thanks be made for all men (1 Tim. 2:1).

When we reflect on God's greatness, we give praise. When we reflect on God's goodness, we give thanks. We humbly express our gratitude for all He has done.

Some people seem to have the idea that it's enough simply to recite the familiar words at mealtime, "God is great, God is good, let us thank Him for our food." To express our genuine gratitude for all of God's goodness, however, certainly takes more time than that! It would take eternity to do it! So, it's not enough to say, "Thanks for the blessings." We must express our appreciation continually for the wonders of salvation, for the joys of life, for the many little things God has done for us, and for the hope that is ours.

The next time you're at the table, don't merely recite the same phrases over and over again. Say something new. Let it come from your heart. And when you enter the private place of prayer, fill some of those moments with sincere expressions of thanks to God.

The Lord is pleased whenever His people tell Him that they are grateful for His blessings. The author of Hebrews wrote:

> Therefore by Him let us continually offer the sacrifice of praise to God, that is, the fruit of our lips, giving thanks to His name (Heb. 13:15).

Yes, express your gratitude to God for the abundant blessings that are yours to enjoy.

CONFESSION

The third essential element of prayer is the confession of our sins to the Lord. Our hearts must be clean and pure when we approach God in prayer. The psalmist said, "If I regard iniquity in my heart, the Lord will not hear" (Ps. 66:18). And you will remember that when Jesus gave us a model prayer, He included the words, "Forgive us our sins."

When we confess our sins, we should be sure to include everything we remember that we did in disobedience to God's will. We should also include our weaknesses, our failures, our omissions, and those sins we may have committed that we aren't even aware of. We must also confess any shortcomings in our personal relationships, be quick to admit that we have failed to exercise faith in God, and acknowledge that we have despised the provision of the Lord. And we must honestly tell God that we have failed Him by compromising with the world.

Yes, we must acknowledge our guilt before God. Then we can claim this promise:

> If we confess our sins, He is faithful and just to forgive us our sins and to cleanse us from all unrighteousness (1 John 1:9).

Prayer is not a place to hide. It is not a front for wrongdoing. Rather, it's a starting point for correcting personal problems. We must think, act, and pray aright. And this calls for confession.

PETITION

Petition is asking for our own needs; intercession is asking for the needs of others. Our petitions should include more than simply asking God to make us better Christians or to provide for our daily needs. Avoiding generalities, we should mention the exact, specific things that we desire for ourselves. Paul wrote:

> Be anxious for nothing, but in everything by prayer and supplication, with thanksgiving, let your requests be made known to God (Phil. 4:6).

We should come to the Lord with all our needs—material and physical, emotional and spiritual, large matters and small. Minor as they may seem to others or even to ourselves, the little things are important to God because He loves us. He's concerned about even the most minute details of our lives.

Even more important, God wants us to do the asking. Jesus said, "Ask, and it will be given to you" (Luke 11:9). But our asking must be properly motivated. James said:

> You ask and do not receive, because you ask amiss, that you may spend it on your pleasures (James 4:3).

Our petitions should also be made in the context of God's will. When we bring Him our requests, let us do so with respect for His knowledge, His timing, and His will. When we ask within the scope of God's will, we can expect the desired answer—and often it's even better than we anticipated. So don't be afraid to be big in your asking. Remember, nothing is impossible with God!

INTERCESSION

Intercession is praying for others. What a ministry can be ours if we will intercede in behalf of our fellow believers or those who are not in God's family! The apostle Paul said, "Brethren, pray for us" (1 Thess. 5:25). Then in 2 Thessalonians he wrote:

> Finally, brethren, pray for us, that the word of the Lord may have free course and be glorified, just as it is with you (2 Thess. 3:1).

In Colossians he spoke of his own prayers for others:

> For this reason we also, since the day we heard it, do not cease to pray for you, and to ask that you may be filled with the knowledge of His will in all wisdom and spiritual understanding (Col. 1:9).

Through intercession we extend our influence into the lives of others. Praying for their needs is a vital element in an effective, God-honoring prayer life. We therefore have an obligation to pray for one another. The ministry of intercession is vital. It is the aspect of our prayers that reaches out to others, and it is both a duty and a privilege.

In this chapter we have reviewed five basic elements of prayer:

Worship
Thanksgiving
Confession
Petition
Intercession

Not every prayer will necessarily include all these elements, but all praying involves one or more of them. And, in time, all of these elements will be a part of your overall prayer life if your prayers are what God intends them to be.

These are a few thoughts about prayer that are very much worth your consideration. The place of prayer is not a catalog office where we simply place orders for the satisfaction of our selfish desires. Prayer is no antidote for inaction. The prayer closet isn't the place to hide from the things in life that need correcting; it's the place to correct them. We must not complain against God if He doesn't answer our prayers the way we think He should—His way is best! Prayer is not twisting God's arm. Rather, we come to Him as to our loving heavenly Father who takes pleasure in giving His children good things. No topic should be considered too mundane. Prayer will make us better Christians. As we pray for others, we will become more loving and less critical. Prayer is a means God has provided for us to talk personally with Him. And through prayer we are given an audience with the Almighty Himself.

Pray thankfully, gratefully acknowledging the privilege of talking with God. Pray thoughtfully, weighing the content of your prayers. Pray expectantly, not fearing to join the disciples in asking, "Lord, teach us to pray." As you put these suggestions into practice, you will find your prayer life more meaningful and more effective. You will be blessed with a sense of God's presence. And you will increase in spiritual power.

Yes, Christian, *pray: God is listening!*

SELF-STUDY

1. What was suggested as a way to worship God with your prayers?

2. In worshiping and thanking God, it is good to (mark *True* or *False*):
   _____ (a) Memorize and repeat the same sentences and phrases.
   _____ (b) Think and say new things in fresh ways.
   _____ (c) Let your prayers become mechanical and perfunctory.

3. a. When we reflect on God's greatness, we give ____________________.

   b. When we reflect on God's goodness, we give ____________________
   ____________________.

4. Several elements we should remember when confessing our sins to the Lord were mentioned. Four of them are:
   a. c.
   b. d.

5. Define each of the following:
   a. Petition.
   b. Intercession.

6. Read Philippians 4:6. What does it say we should pray for? Check the right answer.
   _____ (a) Big, important things.
   _____ (b) Other people's needs only.
   _____ (c) Everything.

Thought Question: What three attitudes were suggested that we should have when praying?

3

How God Answers Prayer

IN THE COURSE of the conversation with his three friends, the afflicted Job stated that wicked people have no regard for God and no use for prayer. According to him, this is what they say:

> Who is the Almighty, that we should serve Him? And what profit do we have if we pray to Him? (Job 21:15).

The unrighteous obviously have no confidence in God, and they see no value whatever in praying to Him.

For a Christian, however, the answer to the question "And what profit do we have if we pray to Him?" is exciting and promising. We know that God hears and answers us whenever we pray.

Elijah prayed and fire came down. The offering on the altar was consumed, and the prophets of Baal were destroyed.

Paul and Silas prayed in prison and the foundations were shaken. The doors were opened and the bonds of all the prisoners were loosened.

Hannah prayed and God gave her a son.

And one of the best-loved psalms contains this promise of

the Lord: "He shall call upon Me, and I will answer him; I will be with him in trouble; I will deliver him and honor him" (Ps. 91:15).

Yes, my friend, God answers prayer! The poet Eliza Hickok wrote:

> I know not by what methods rare,
> But this I know, God answers prayer.
> I know not when He sends the word
> That tells us fervent prayer is heard.
> I know it cometh soon or late:
> Therefore we need to pray and wait.
> I know not if the blessing sought
> Will come in just the guise I thought.
> I leave my prayers with Him alone
> Whose will is wiser than my own.

Even though these statements about prayer are true, sometimes it seems as if God's ears are deaf and the heavens above are made of brass. Our desperate cries appear to go no higher than the ceiling. Why is this? If God does hear and answer prayer, how can we explain those occasions when nothing seems to happen, when there is no apparent answer, when our troubles increase rather than go away, and when we're tempted to doubt the very promises of God?

I believe the answer lies in the fact that God does respond to all believers' prayers, but that He does so in different ways. In this chapter, let's look at three of them: yes, no, and wait. As we look at each of them, I trust that you will understand prayer more fully and improve your own prayer life. I pray that even if your answers aren't exactly what you wanted, you'll learn to rest with confidence in the wisdom of our all-knowing God.

GOD MAY ANSWER "YES"

One way God answers our prayers is by giving us what we ask for. His answer is yes. An incident in the life of King Hezekiah is an example:

> In those days Hezekiah was sick and near death. And Isaiah the prophet, the son of Amoz, went to him and said to him, "Thus says the Lord: Set your house in order, for you shall die, and not live."

> Then he turned his face toward the wall, and prayed to the Lord, saying,
>
> "Remember now, O Lord, I pray, how I have walked before You in truth and with a loyal heart, and have done what was good in Your sight." And Hezekiah wept bitterly.
>
> Then it happened, before Isaiah had gone out into the middle court, that the word of the Lord came to him, saying,
>
> "Return and tell Hezekiah the leader of My people, 'Thus says the Lord, the God of David your father: "I have heard your prayer, I have seen your tears; surely I will heal you. On the third day you shall go up to the house of the Lord.
>
> "And I will add to your days fifteen years. I will deliver you and this city from the hand of the king of Assyria; and I will defend this city for My own sake, and for the sake of My servant David."'" (2 Kings 20:1–6).

According to verse 1, Hezekiah was "sick and near death." In fact, God had already told him to set his house in order. But the good king cried to the Lord in prayer, and God responded by saying, "I have heard your prayer, I have seen your tears; surely I will heal you." God certainly does answer prayer—often with a yes!

God sometimes gives us a bigger yes than we expected. He not only told Hezekiah that He would heal him, but He went on to say:

> And I will add to your days fifteen years. I will deliver you and this city from the hand of the king of Assyria; and I will defend this city for My own sake, and for the sake of My servant David (2 Kings 20:6).

We aren't told exactly what Hezekiah prayed for, but we can be quite certain that he asked for healing. God not only granted that request, but He went on to do much more. The Lord promised Hezekiah that He would add fifteen years to his life, that He would deliver Jerusalem from the Assyrians, and that He Himself would defend the city. God did much more for Hezekiah than simply heal his body!

Paul told us in Ephesians that God "is able to do

exceedingly abundantly above all that we ask or think, according to the power that works in us" (Eph. 3:20). What a comfort to know that God answers prayer! What a blessing to realize that sometimes He says yes with such timeliness, bestowal of inner peace, and expression of His love that we are overwhelmed with His presence and goodness.

GOD MAY ANSWER "NO"

The second way God may answer our prayers is by saying no to what we have requested. There are times when God, according to His own wisdom and will, refuses to grant us our desires. He may do so for a number of reasons. If the one who prays is an unbeliever, for example, he can have no assurance that the Lord will give him the desires of his heart. The man born blind, but who was healed by Christ, spoke the truth when he said:

> Now we know that God does not hear sinners; but if anyone is a worshiper of God and does His will, He hears him (John 9:31).

Also, we cannot expect our prayers to be effective unless we are living in fellowship with the Lord. Jesus said, "If you abide in Me, and My words abide in you, you will ask what you desire, and it shall be done for you" (John 15:7). And the psalmist said, "If I regard iniquity in my heart, the Lord will not hear" (Ps. 66:18).

Our prayers are also answered with a no when we ask with wrong motives. James warned, "You ask and do not receive, because you ask amiss, that you may spend it on your pleasures" (James 4:3).

Sometimes our prayers receive a negative response because they are not in accordance with God's will. The Bible says, "Now this is the confidence that we have in Him, that if we ask anything according to His will, He hears us" (1 John 5:14). It stands to reason, then, that if we do not pray according to the will of God, He will not grant our requests.

Remember, the Lord may say no when we ask, but it's always for our benefit. Even so, if we ask something and do not receive it, God's refusal is in reality an answer to our prayer. I like the way Lehman Strauss put it in his book, *Sense and Nonsense About Prayer.*

> When God says no, that is an answer. It is a denial. Many Christians do not have an understanding of this kind of answer to prayer. They simply complain that God did not answer.

An example in the Bible of God's no to our requests can be found in the experience of the prophet Elijah. When wicked Queen Jezebel threatened to kill him, the prophet cried out for God to take his life. But this was not the Lord's will for him. Instead, God miraculously provided for Elijah's physical needs, then later took him by a whirlwind into heaven (2 Kings 2:11).

At times the Lord denies the things we ask for. But He knows what's best. If He does not grant us our petitions, and if we know our hearts are right with Him, we should simply trust Him and depend on Him to meet our needs. He is always faithful in doing so. The apostle Paul knew this, for he wrote:

> And lest I should be exalted above measure by the abundance of the revelations, a thorn in the flesh was given to me, a messenger of Satan to buffet me, lest I should be exalted above measure.
>
> Concerning this thing I pleaded with the Lord three times that it might depart from me.
>
> And He said to me, "My grace is sufficient for you, for My strength is made perfect in weakness." Therefore, most gladly I will rather boast in my infirmities, that the power of Christ may rest upon me (2 Cor. 12:7-9).

Paul asked the Lord three times to remove his "thorn in the flesh." What did God do? He denied Paul's request. He said no. But He met his need, giving Paul sufficient grace to bear his affliction. And Paul was willing to glorify God through it.

We must also remember that when God says no to our petitions, He may substitute something far better. His choice is always the best. Henry Bosch told this story in *Our Daily Bread*:

> A certain man lived so far from a store that he sent for his clothing by mail. At the bottom of the printed order form he would always see the words, "If we don't have the article you ordered in stock, may we substitute?" He

> remembered that on one occasion when he wrote yes, he got something that was worth double the price of the article requested. Along with it came a note that said, "We are sorry that we do not have the article in stock that you ordered; therefore, we are sending you something better at our expense!" After that, the man said he always printed the word "yes" very plainly at the bottom of the order blank. He knew he would not be disappointed in their substitution.

When we pray to God, it's wise for us to include the yes on the bottom of our "order form," indicating our willingness to let Him change our prayers according to His will. We know that He could send something better, something "exceedingly abundantly above all that we ask or think" (Eph. 3:20).

GOD MAY ANSWER "WAIT"

There is a third way that God may answer our prayers. He may say *yes*, He may say *no*, or He may say *wait*. Our request may be right, but the timing may be wrong. The Lord knows that conditions aren't just right, so He may put us in a "holding pattern."

I'm sure that every one of us at some time or other has earnestly prayed for something. It may have been for the fulfillment of a cherished dream, or for a loved one's salvation. We thought the answer would never come. But finally, in God's own time, our request was granted. As we look back, we can thank God for not saying yes sooner. In the process of waiting we learned to rest and trust, and we learned not to wrestle with God.

Sometimes the waiting is good for us. We are taught, nurtured, and strengthened as God accomplishes His righteous purpose. The poet has written:

> Unanswered yet! No, do not say ungranted;
> Perhaps your part is not yet fully done.
> The work began when first your prayer was raised,
> God will finish what He has begun.
> If you will keep faith's incense burning there,
> His glory you shall see sometime, somewhere.

My friend, God does answer prayer. Sometimes He says *yes* and gives us what we ask for—even more and better than we expected. But sometimes the answer is *no,* for He knows that what we asked for isn't good for us. Sometimes God's answer is *wait*. He wants us to learn patience and to trust Him more fully. But we can be certain that whatever He does, it's for our benefit and blessing. When we understand and believe this, when we come to Him expectantly, we can rejoice in His answers. And we can remain strong in hope.

Pray: God is listening! He answers prayer!

SELF-STUDY

1. What happened when
   a. Elijah prayed?
   b. Paul and Silas prayed?
   c. Hannah prayed?

2. What two things does the answer to Hezekiah's prayer tell us about God's response to prayer?
   a.
   b.

3. Name four reasons God may say no to prayer.
   a.
   b.
   c.
   d.

4. When God answers no to our prayers, it is because (mark *True* or *False*):
   _____ (a) He is cruel and vindictive.
   _____ (b) He knows what is best for us.
   _____ (c) He is capricious and whimsical.

Thought Question: How have you responded when God said no to one of your prayers?

5. Can you think of two reasons God's answers to our prayers may be *wait?*
   a.
   b.

Challenge Question: Can you tell the difference between *no* and *wait* answers to your prayers?

4

Hindrances to Prayer

DURING THE PAST two decades we have witnessed an increasing emphasis on the value of effective communication. We are being urged to verbalize our feelings. Many people today, unable to engage in a satisfactory dialogue with relatives or friends, are talking over their problems and discussing their deepest fears, loves, and hates with their ministers, counselors, and psychiatrists. Thousands are attending combined therapy sessions where, under the direction of trained counselors, they share their thoughts and emotions with others who have similar difficulties. In addition to these outlets for expression, small groups gather to voice their religious aspirations, their anxieties, and their hopes. Yes, a lot of attention is being given to vocalizing our most intimate concerns.

But we aren't hearing much about the importance of talking with God. This vertical relationship that we have with the Almighty is more needful than any of the others. Yet, sad to say, prayerlessness is all too common—among Christians as well as unbelievers.

"Oh," I can hear someone say, "don't most believers pray when they rise in the morning, at mealtime, and before they go to bed at night?" Yes, I suppose they do. But I wonder, how many know what it is to have genuine fellowship with God? How many truly talk with Him as their heavenly Father? If the facts were known, I'm afraid we would find that many Christians are simply going through a ritualistic recitation of words while their eyes are closed and their hands are folded. But how often are they really engaging in a meaningful, personal communication with the Lord?

What is the reason for this ineffectiveness in prayer? Why are so many of God's children neglecting one of life's greatest privileges? And when they do pray, why are their petitions offered in such a cold, mechanical, and faithless manner? I can think of a number of reasons. In this chapter I would like to discuss two of them. They are actually theological issues, and they have perplexed and troubled God's children down through the years to the point of affecting their prayer life.

These two questions were expressed in the following letter from a Radio Bible Class listener:

> I know the Bible exhorts us to pray and that Jesus and the apostles were men of prayer. But why is God so concerned about our praying? After all, He is sovereign. He knows everything from the beginning to the end. How can it be true that prayer changes things when "what's to be will be"? All the details of a person's life have been decreed. Besides, it seems that God, who is infinite in love and holiness, would do what is best for us without our begging Him. So why does He command us to thank and praise Him, and confess our sins? He's well aware of the sorrow we experience because of our sins. Why then is it so necessary to tell Him about these things and to ask Him for our human needs?

As we discuss the two questions raised in this letter, I trust that it will clarify matters, and that you will be influenced to become more effective in your own life of prayer.

WHY PRAY TO A SOVEREIGN GOD?

The first question, simply stated, is this: If God is sovereign and knows ahead of time everything that is going to happen, why should we even bother to pray? That's a good question. It demands a response.

As we search for the answer to the question of how the power of prayer relates to the sovereignty of God, we should be careful not to deny that the Lord does have a plan for this earth and for those who love Him. Referring to believers, the apostle Paul said:

> In whom [Christ] also we have obtained an inheritance, being predestined according to the purpose of Him who works all things according to the counsel of His will (Eph. 1:11).

The truth of God's sovereignty, however, must not be confused with fatalism. Nowhere does the Bible deny man's responsibility. The Scriptures never encourage carelessness, nor do they belittle the value of prayer.

I am reminded of a story told by the outstanding theologian A. H. Strong. In order to emphasize the fallacy of blind determinism, he related an imaginary instance of a man who lived in the horse-and-buggy days. One Sunday, after hearing a sermon at church about God's sovereignty, he took a rough, shorter trail home instead of the longer, safer route. The way was filled with ruts and rocks. When a wagon wheel finally broke, he made this stupid observation: "I have been predestined to be a fool, and I have just made my calling and election sure." This poor person did not realize that his own free action had been foreseen and incorporated into God's plan.

In the same way, the person who doesn't pray because he concludes that things are foreknown anyway is overlooking the fact that God, in His omniscience, foresaw his own prayerlessness. Don't forget, the Lord's eternal foreknowledge took our prayers into consideration. He has worked them into His plan and into the very fabric of the universe! That's why we pray, even though we acknowledge God's sovereignty and the existence of His plans.

I like the way James Oliver Buswell illustrated this idea. He pointed out that parents, even with limited foresight, can often anticipate their children's needs. Because they do, they make advance preparations. If a youngster is feverish in the evening, for example, his mother will be quite sure that he will call for her during the night. So before she goes to bed, she checks to see if proper medications and other provisions are on hand. She has anticipated his cry and is ready to meet the need. When we apply this to the spiritual realm, we conclude that from all eternity God knew the exact situations in which we would find ourselves. He knew how we would respond. So, knowing full well whether or not we would pray, He made His all-wise plans and provisions for an answer. We can therefore accept at face value the gracious prayer invitations of the Bible. Jesus said:

> Ask, and it will be given to you; seek, and you will find; knock, and it will be opened to you.
>
> For everyone who asks receives, and he who seeks finds, and to him who knocks it will be opened.
>
> Or what man is there among you who, if his son asks for bread, will give him a stone?
>
> Or if he asks for a fish, will he give him a serpent?
>
> If you then, being evil, know how to give good gifts to your children, how much more will your Father who is in heaven give good things to those who ask Him! (Matt. 7:7–11).

No, don't let a wrong concept of God's sovereignty discourage you from praying. Remember, the Lord's plans are not formed on the basis of blind fate. Rather, they have been conceived in the mind of a loving, all-knowing God who has foreseen our prayers and has already made provision for their answers. It really is true that prayer changes things.

WHY PRAY TO AN OMNISCIENT GOD?

The second question raised about prayer in the letter I quoted earlier relates to God's omniscience. Since the Lord is all-knowing, why is it necessary to express our needs to Him, to thank Him for all His blessings, and to confess our sins? After all, He knows our situation. He knows the gratitude in our hearts. And He knows without our telling Him the depth of our sorrow for sin. Therefore, what is the value and purpose of praying to an omniscient God?

In answering, we should remember that the possibility of prayer should be a source of great comfort to believers. The very fact that God wants us to talk to Him should tell us that He loves us. It should convince us that He looks on our feelings, our needs, and our desires as important. Otherwise He wouldn't have told us to pray. It's not that our heavenly Father wants to hear us say *please, thank You,* and *I'm sorry* just to satisfy His own ego. As the infinite Creator, with millions of angels praising and serving Him, what could we add to His glory? God listens to us because He cares for us. It is therefore primarily for our benefit that we are to pray. Through speaking with Him we are brought to the place where we keenly feel His presence and become deeply conscious of His love.

Think, for example, of the relationship that exists between a father and his son. When the boy fails to make the football team, when he is having difficulty with his studies, or when the girl he is dating turns to someone else, the loving father senses his son's discouragement and tries in every way possible to get him to talk. You see, he really loves that child. He knows that a heart-to-heart talk would be of tremendous help. No, it wouldn't put him on the football team. And it wouldn't return his former girl friend. But it would reassure him of his father's love, and it would give him a much better view of the entire situation. The young man could then make the needed adjustments in his thinking and face the future with new courage and anticipation. A talk with dad can do wonders!

Likewise, our heavenly Father wants us to speak to Him. If we do, we can enjoy a wonderful awareness of His presence and maintain a spirit of gladness and hope even in the unpleasant situations of life. When we know that God is near, and when we have the confidence that His will is always best, we can face life's trials with optimism and courage.

God wants us to delight in the blessed reality of His nearness. He loves us. He takes pleasure in listening to us. And when we talk to Him, He imparts to us a sense of His personal presence. Tennyson expressed this truth beautifully when he wrote:

> Speak to Him thou, speak to Him thou,
>   For He hears, and spirit with Spirit can meet—
> Closer is He than breathing,
>   And nearer than hands and feet.

Yes, friend, *Pray: God is listening!*

Even though prayer is a wonderful privilege, it is also a solemn obligation. God wants you to talk to Him. He wants to impart to you the sense of His presence. So don't neglect the opportunity to come before Him. Don't deprive yourself of the best He has for you. Tennyson expressed it well:

> More things are wrought by prayer than this world
>   dreams of.
> Wherefore, let thy voice rise like a fountain for me
>   night and day.
> For what are men better than sheep and goats
>   That nourish a blind life within the brain,
> If, knowing God, they lift not hands in prayer
>   Both for themselves and those who call them friends?
> For so the whole round earth is every way
>   Bound by gold chains about the feet of God.

THE DOOR IS OPEN TO YOU

Only those who know the Lord through faith in Christ can enjoy the privilege of talking to, communing with, and expecting answers from the Father in heaven. If you have never received the Lord Jesus by faith as your personal Savior, why not do so today?

SELF-STUDY

1. Before beginning, take a moment to think about your prayer life. Write down some things that keep you from praying as you should.

2. We discussed two theological questions that sometimes keep people from praying. They are:
   a.
   b.

3. Read the section, "Why pray to a sovereign God?" and mark the following statements *True* or *False*.
   ____ (a) God has a plan for all who love Him.
   ____ (b) God's sovereignty is the same as fatalism.
   ____ (c) The Bible does not emphasize man's responsibility to pray.
   ____ (d) The Lord's foreknowledge took our prayers into consideration.
   ____ (e) Prayer changes things.

4. Why are we commanded to pray?
   ____ (a) For God's benefit.
   ____ (b) For our own benefit.
   ____ (c) To satisfy God's ego.

Suggestion: Memorize Matthew 7:7–11, and quote it whenever you get discouraged about prayer.

5

What Shall I Say?

WHEN SOME CHRISTIANS think about talking with God and realize that it's not simply a matter of "saying their prayers," they become apprehensive and bewildered. This is especially true for those who learned in their homes or were instructed in churches to go through the motions of repeating memorized prayers, but never progressed in communicating with the Lord beyond this point. The idea of conversing with the Lord in a spontaneous manner frightens them. They wonder, "How do I address God?" "In what manner should I approach Him?" "What should I say?"

If this describes your situation, it will help you to know that the disciples faced the very same problem. On one occasion they came to Jesus, saying, "Lord, teach us to pray" (Luke 11:1). He responded by giving them the prayer recorded in Luke and in Matthew.

> So He said to them, "When you pray, say: Our Father in heaven, hallowed be Your name. Your kingdom come. Your will be done on earth as it is in heaven. Give us day by day our daily bread. And forgive us our sins, for we

also forgive everyone who is indebted to us. And do not lead us into temptation, but deliver us from the evil one" (Luke 11:2–4).

This prayer was designed to be a pattern of how to talk with God. In our study of the model prayer, we will consider phrase by phrase the basic elements involved in successfully communing with our heavenly Father, with the earnest hope that your prayer life will become more effective. Please notice first, however, that the opening words, "Our Father in heaven," produce in us a sense of intimacy and a feeling of reverence.

INTIMACY

How beautifully the words "Our Father" express the closeness of our relationship to God! We are to call Him *Father*. In a home where the father has a good relationship with his children, the little ones feel security and contentment. They know that they were loved even before they could express any affection in return. They are confident that their father's concern and interest takes in, with one large embrace, all the small and great things in their lives. They feel assured that his love will not diminish just because they have been disobedient. Yes, Dad may chasten them when they do wrong and deserve his punishment, but as a loving father his heart always yearns for the quick reestablishment of a close and warm relationship.

All who have received the Lord Jesus can come to God with this same assurance, since He is our heavenly Father. This is a privilege that only believers can enjoy. No one else has that right. Oh, I know that all people, as Paul said in his sermon from Mars Hill, are the "offspring of God" (Acts 17:29). And Jesus made it clear in Matthew 5:45 that the Almighty shows a loving concern for all mankind in that "He makes His sun rise on the evil and on the good, and sends rain on the just and on the unjust." Even though these things are true, the only people qualified to say "Our Father in heaven" are those who have been redeemed through faith in the Lord Jesus Christ.

The apostle John has told us that we become members of God's family at conversion.

> But as many as received Him, to them He gave the right to become children of God, even to those who believe in His name (John 1:12).

This precious family relationship is also expressed in John's first epistle, where the apostle repeatedly referred to believers as "little children." The new birth makes us members of the household of God.

Paul referred to our sonship and the privileges it brings when he said:

> For as many as are led by the Spirit of God, these are sons of God.
>
> For you did not receive the spirit of bondage again to fear, but you received the Spirit of adoption by whom we cry out, "Abba, Father."
>
> The Spirit Himself bears witness with our spirit that we are children of God, and if children, then heirs—heirs of God and joint heirs with Christ, if indeed we suffer with Him, that we may also be glorified together (Rom. 8:14–17).

Think of it, friend! You and I who have received God's Son, the Lord Jesus Christ, can now address the Almighty as "Father," and we can enjoy all the legal rights of sonship. Every time we pray, we should be overwhelmed with gratitude for the privilege of saying, *"Our Father* in heaven." He is our heavenly Father, and this should give us a beautiful sense of intimacy when we pray.

REVERENCE

We are also to approach the Lord with deep reverence because of His holiness. Our feeling of closeness to the Lord must never lead to disrespect or an overly familiar attitude. Jesus told us to say, "Our Father *in heaven*." We must remember that God is in heaven; we are on earth. He is infinite in holiness and power; *we* are sinful and weak. Let us never think of Him as merely "the Man upstairs." Yes, He is our Father, and what a blessed relationship! But He is "Our Father *in heaven*." Oh, the marvel of His condescending grace!

Having pointed out that we come to God as His children but must maintain a sense of deep reverence, we are now ready for the question, What should I say when I talk with God? The prayer suggested by our Lord sets forth five different petitions that should be of significant help in guiding us when we pray: (1) Hallowed be Your name; (2) Your kingdom come; Your will be done on earth as it is in heaven; (3) Give us day by day our daily bread; (4) Forgive us our sins; (5) Do not lead us into temptation.

HALLOWED BE YOUR NAME

The first phrase suggested by our Lord when addressing God as our heavenly Father is "Hallowed be Your name." God's name is to be honored above all other names. When you pray like this with sincerity and with a genuine desire for the realization of your request, you will find yourself praising the Lord for His majesty and glory. You will thank Him for His blessedness. And you will intercede for erring believers, for all of God's servants, and for the lost.

When you talk to God, don't merely repeat the words, "Hallowed be Your name." Instead, using language of your own, offer Him your praises, sincerely express your innermost thoughts and wishes, and intercede for the spiritual needs of others. Whenever believers pray this way, God's name is truly "hallowed."

YOUR KINGDOM COME

The second request in our Lord's model prayer should reflect our earnest longing for that coming day when the rule of God will be universally acknowledged. We live in a world marred by sin. It is largely under the influence of Satan, who is called in the Bible "the god of this age." We are distressed by what we see all about us, yet we know that this earth will never see worldwide peace, universal righteousness, or absolute justice until the Lord Jesus returns and establishes His reign. Our hearts cry out, "Your kingdom come. Your will be done on earth as it is in heaven." We yearn for the fulfillment of the time foretold by Jeremiah:

> "Behold, the days are coming," says the Lord, "that I will raise to David a Branch of righteousness; a King shall reign and prosper, and execute judgment and righteous-

> ness in the earth. In His days Judah will be saved, and Israel will dwell safely; now this is His name by which He will be called: The Lord Our Righteousness" (Jer. 23:5–6).

God's will is done perfectly now in heaven, and when Christ comes again it will be the same here on earth. Our prayers should therefore express a longing for the return of Christ, and we should say with the apostle John, "Even so, come, Lord Jesus!" (Rev. 22:20).

The fact that the petition "Your kingdom come, Your will be done on earth as it is in heaven" is essentially a request for the establishment of God's kingdom does not mean that we should be indifferent to present conditions. On the contrary, we want the Lord's will to be done here and now. We have a deep longing in our hearts that men and women everywhere would acknowledge Jesus Christ as Lord of Lords and King of Kings. For that reason, we should pray for all men in positions of leadership, for the needy, and for a measure of peace and prosperity throughout the world. Paul said:

> Therefore I exhort first of all that supplications, prayers, intercessions, and giving of thanks be made for all men, for kings and all who are in authority, that we may lead a quiet and peaceable life in all godliness and reverence (1 Tim. 2:1–2).

GIVE US . . . DAILY BREAD

The third petition Jesus taught His followers was "Give us day by day our daily bread." This is a request for God to meet our physical requirements. The Bible makes it clear that our heavenly Father recognizes our need for food, clothing, and protection from the elements. As physical beings in a material world, we are confronted continually with the necessity of replenishing our dwindling strength and diminishing resources. So take comfort in God's concern, for these things are not unimportant to Him. He does want us to have our values properly placed, however, and to live in conscious dependence on Him. He is pleased when we trust Him for the necessities of life. God wants us to be willing to live one day at a time. Jesus said, "Give us *day by day* our *daily* bread."

Christian friend, God has made us individual human

beings in a physical world. He knows that we need food and clothing, and that life is enjoyed most when we possess good health and enough material things to give us more than bare existence. He wants us as His children to talk to Him every day about our basic needs. And you know, I don't think He frowns when you ask Him for something a little extra. Remember, He loves you. He knows all about your circumstances, and He cares.

FORGIVE US OUR SINS

Our Lord not only instructed us in His model prayer to ask for our *physical* needs, but He also included a request related to our *spiritual* well-being. He told His disciples to say, "and forgive us our sins; for we also forgive everyone who is indebted to us." Jesus was not talking here about an unsaved person coming to God for pardon, but the confession of sin by a Christian that he might experience a blessed and continued fellowship with God.

You see, the Lord doesn't go to an unsaved person and say, "I will justify you, but *only* if you forgive others." He forgives and receives the sinner when he believes on Christ. *After* we have become the children of God, however, we can enjoy a close walk and fellowship with Him only as we confess our sins every day and willingly forgive those who have wronged us. We cannot expect to enjoy the blessing of God's peace and presence if we harbor an unforgiving spirit toward those who have treated us unjustly. Every time we pray, we should be conscious of our sins and confess them to the Lord. But we must also search our innermost beings and make certain we have a right attitude toward others. Most pastors can testify that they have known Christians who were miserable because they carried the terrible burden of a guilty conscience. They were delivered, however, when they confessed their sins to the Lord and were willing to forgive those toward whom they felt a deep resentment.

The Lord Jesus in Matthew 5:23–24 underscored the importance of having a forgiving spirit. He emphasized the fact that if someone has brought his gift to the altar and there remembers that he has bitter feelings toward a fellowman, he should leave the place of sacrifice and be reconciled to the hated brother before presenting his offering. If we all talked with God daily, confessing our sins and cleansing our hearts of hatred and resentment, we wouldn't have as many ulcers, unhappy homes, or divided churches.

DO NOT LEAD US INTO TEMPTATION

The final petition in the disciples' prayer is, "And do not lead us into temptation, but deliver us from the evil one."

The Greek word translated "temptation" can mean a solicitation to evil, or a trial that one must endure. As a Christian, I know that times of testing are part and parcel of my earthly life. I'm always going to be tempted by my old nature, the world-system, and Satan. I'm also sure to meet disappointments, pain, and unpleasant situations along the way. But I should not let this knowledge cause me to become a fatalist. I should never say, "Well, what will be will be. If I have to suffer, then I'll just have to suffer. If temptations come, I'll stand up to them. But I won't ask God for any relief, nor expect any special help." No, I should ask for exemption from trials and deliverance from evil.

Such requests must always be made in a spirit of humble submission to the will of God, however. In the Garden of Gethsemane, Jesus reacted with abhorrence to the ordeal of bearing God's wrath against sin. He even asked the Father to remove the cup of suffering from Him. But then He added, "Nevertheless not My will, but Yours, be done" (Luke 22:42). The apostle Paul said that on three different occasions he asked the Lord to remove "a thorn in the flesh, . . . a messenger of Satan," from which he longed for deliverance. (See 2 Cor. 12:7–8.) But when God told him, "My grace is sufficient for you, for My strength is made perfect in weakness" (2 Cor. 12:9), Paul submitted to the will of God and accepted his trial without complaining.

Following the examples of Jesus and Paul by asking the Lord for favorable situations when difficulties come our way, we should accept God's will for our lives. Then, looking to Him for strength and realizing the presence of the indwelling Holy Spirit, we can effectively meet whatever challenges may confront us.

Let me ask you: Do you talk with God? Is it a regular practice? What do you say to Him? As we've seen in this chapter, the Lord Jesus Himself has given us clear guidelines. The "disciples' prayer" of Luke 11 provides a pattern and an outline for effective communication with the Lord. It was not given, however, to be rattled off word for word, repetitiously and mechanically, every Sunday in a formalized worship situation. Instead, this prayer should help and encourage us as we open our hearts and in our own words share our burdens, needs, and innermost longings with our heavenly Father.

As you talk to the Lord with intimacy and reverence, remember first of all to praise Him for His greatness, His love, and His goodness. Then, as you think of this sin-sick world and find yourself yearning for that day when Christ's righteous rule will be established, express your longing for His return. Intercede for all who are in positions of authority, and for the poor and oppressed of the earth. Ask God for the measure of peace, righteousness, and prosperity consistent with His will for today. Leave tomorrow in His hands. Be honest in confessing your sins, and make sure you forgive all who have wronged you. Finally, acknowledge your weakness and your need to depend on the Lord. Ask Him to lead you where you will not be tempted to sin. Remember that your heavenly Father is perfect in wisdom, power, and love. Let the words "Not *my* will but Yours be done" permeate all your praying.

SELF-STUDY

1. What attitude do you think we should take when we approach God?
   _____ (a) Always with formal address.
   _____ (b) Informal, as we would talk to our friends.
   _____ (c) In the manner the situation demands.

2. The Lord's Prayer begins with the words "Our Father." What does this title suggest to you?

3. Who has the privilege of truly addressing God as "our Father"?

4. What aspect of God's character do the words "in heaven" suggest?

5. What does it mean to "hallow" God's name?

Challenge Question: Does the verse beginning "Your kingdom come" apply to today or only to the future?

6. What is the principal meaning of "Give us . . . our daily bread"? "Forgive us our sins"?

7. What two elements are implied by the words "and do not lead us into temptation"?

Suggestion: The next time you pray (perhaps right now), try to include the five petitions mentioned in this chapter.

6

What If God Doesn't Answer?

THE BIBLE IS emphatic in its teaching that God answers prayer. When the Israelites were in a state of desperation in the wilderness, Moses talked to the Lord about the bitterness of the drinking water, and God miraculously made it sweet. The barren Hannah asked the Lord for a child, and Samuel was born to her. Elijah asked Jehovah to demonstrate His superiority over Baal, and fire came down from heaven. Hezekiah prayed when he was dying, and the Lord added 15 years to his life. Christian friends interceded for Peter when he was in prison awaiting execution, and an angel delivered him. Jesus promised, "Ask, and it will be given to you; seek, and you will find; knock, and it will be opened to you" (Matt. 7:7). James declared, "The effective, fervent prayer of a righteous man avails much" (James 5:16). Yes, the Bible clearly teaches that the Lord always hears His people when they pray, and thousands today will give ready testimony that God has heard and responded to their petitions. Every Christian who walks in fellowship with the Lord knows the truth of the statement, "Satan laughs at our toiling, mocks at our wisdom, but trembles when we pray."

But the Lord doesn't always give us everything we ask for.

In fact, at times it appears that He doesn't even hear us. Whenever this happens, some believers become deeply disturbed. They wonder if God still loves them, or if their prayers cannot be answered. Still others continue to pray but don't really believe that anything will happen. They keep on talking to God, but only in a general way. They offer thanks and make requests out of duty, never becoming very specific. Yes, they believe that Romans 8:28 is true when it says that everything will work out for good in their lives, but somehow they have lost confidence in the power of prayer. This is a tragedy whenever it occurs.

What do you do when heaven seems closed, and there's no apparent response or answer to the earnest pleas of your burdened heart? In this chapter we will take a look at the entire matter of unanswered prayer. Let me suggest five steps every believer should take when he encounters this problem: (1) Engage in self-examination; (2) Reaffirm your relationship to God; (3) Acknowledge His infinity; (4) Submit to His will; (5) Keep on praying.

SELF-EXAMINATION

The first step is to engage in self-examination. It is possible that some sin in your life is standing between you and the blessing of God. The psalmist declared, "If I regard iniquity in my heart, the Lord will not hear" (Ps. 66:18). Isaiah sounded the same note, saying:

> But your iniquities have separated you from your God;
> and your sins have hidden His face from you (Isa. 59:2).

Therefore, earnestly search your own heart. If you really mean business, you can be certain that the Holy Spirit will quickly show you your sin. When He does, confess it, and accept God's full forgiveness. The Bible says:

> If we confess our sins, He is faithful and just to forgive us our sins and to cleanse us from all unrighteousness (1 John 1:9).

Then too, you may discover that you have been praying selfishly, petitioning God with the wrong motives. James put his finger on this possibility when he wrote, "You ask and do not receive, because you ask amiss, that you may spend it on your pleasures" (James 4:3). It is really surprising, and sometimes shocking, to realize how self-centered we can be in our praying. The mother of James and John, for example, asked the Lord Jesus to give her sons the two top positions in His future kingdom. That was certainly a selfish request! But before judging her too harshly, remember that many of our prayers are just as self-seeking. Let us examine our hearts and make sure we are not selfishly motivated in our prayers.

REAFFIRM OUR RELATIONSHIP TO GOD

If it seems that God doesn't respond to our prayers, we should reaffirm our relationship to Him. It is easy for us to allow our feelings to take control, even to the extent that we forget the "family" relationship we have with God through our faith in the Lord Jesus Christ. At these times we must go to the Bible and rest on its message. It tells us that God has proven His love for us, and assures us that through faith in the death, burial, and resurrection of Christ we have been made children of the Father. With such a knowledge, we never need to allow the forces of Satan or our own emotions to shake our confidence in His love for us.

The importance of recognizing that our relationship to God is based on what He has done in Christ cannot be overemphasized. When our prayers are not answered in the way we expect, it's quite easy to become discouraged and allow our feelings to sway us. When that happens, we could become vulnerable to statements that would turn prayer into some kind of magical gimmick. Some people make frantic appeals to religious organizations, or seek other means to manipulate God. They will send for a prayer card, or place their hands on the radio or television set while some preacher who purports to have a special gift leads in prayer.

But listen, friend, when a believer resorts to special ceremonies, or puts confidence in objects of *supposed* efficacy, or continuously repeats certain phrases, he is forgetting his relationship with his heavenly Father. Jesus said:

> But when you pray, do not use vain repetitions as the heathen do. For they think that they will be heard for their many words.
>
> Therefore do not be like them. For your Father knows the things you have need of before you ask Him (Matt. 6:7–8).

The Lord has proven His love for you in sending His Son. When you trusted Christ, God became your heavenly Father. He is a person, not some kind of mystical power to be manipulated if you can only hit upon the right formula. You can freely come to Him in this confidence!

ACKNOWLEDGE GOD'S INFINITY

A third step you can take when your prayers seem unanswered is to acknowledge God's infinite goodness, His wisdom, and His greatness. He is all-powerful, all-knowing, and all-loving. An awareness of this can comfort and encourage your heart as you face the disappointments of unanswered prayer. You can be certain that God has a special reason for His refusal, and that it is consistent with His boundless wisdom and infinite love.

Our knowledge is extremely limited and we sometimes ask for things that are not good for us. So, it is really a blessing that God denies some of our requests. I like the statement of Jean Ingelow, who said, "I have lived to thank God that not all of my prayers have been answered."

We must also realize that even when everything seems to be going wrong, the Lord, who sees the end from the beginning, may actually be working all things for our good. He often allows a request to go seemingly unheeded in order to bring us even greater blessing than we asked for. This can be illustrated by an experience in the life of Augustine. One day he set sail for Rome at the very same time that his mother, Monica, was pleading with God to keep him home. It must have seemed to her that the Lord was ignoring her prayer, but it was through that very journey that her illustrious son was converted. Augustine commented later on God's mysterious ways when he wrote, "But Thou in Thy hidden wisdom didst grant the substance of her desire. Ye refused the thing she prayed for, in order that

Thou mightest effect in me what she was ever praying for. . . . She loved to keep me with her as mothers are wont, yes, far more than most mothers, and she knew not what joy Thou wast preparing for her out of my desertion." The Lord knew what He was doing when He refused Monica's plea. She had prayed that her son might be kept from going to Rome, but God allowed him to go, and made the journey that broke his mother's heart the occasion for Augustine's conversion. In the same way, God may be denying some of your heart's deepest desires. But He might well be doing something for you that will transcend all your present longings.

SUBMIT TO GOD'S WILL

After acknowledging the Lord's perfection and our own sinfulness and frailty, we should submit fully and gladly to the will of God. When I pause to meditate on what God is like, I am fully assured that His ways are designed for my greatest good, and that the wisest thing I can do is to say, "Not my will, but Yours, be done." It is both sinful and dangerous to pray any other way. The Israelites learned this truth in the wilderness. They should have been grateful to God, for He had delivered them from slavery in Egypt. He also was sustaining them with manna and was working many marvelous miracles for them. But they began to complain bitterly and begged the Lord for meat. So He answered their prayers by sending great flocks of quail they could easily kill and eat. The Scriptures tell us, however, that God also sent a plague on them, and that a large number of the Israelites died while they were still eating. The inspired psalmist, commenting on this tragedy, declared:

> He gave them their request, but sent leanness into their soul (Ps. 106:15).

I sometimes wonder how many of the sorrows of our lives are the result of self-willed prayers. The Lord may give us our requests, but they turn out to be a curse rather than a blessing. How much better to say, "Not my will, but Yours, be done." The Lord's way may not always be easy. We might go through all of life without ever knowing the reason he has refused one of our petitions. But we can be absolutely certain that His way is best, and that He will surely meet our deepest needs. Whenever we completely trust the Lord and submit to Him, we receive enabling grace, special strength, and a consciousness of God's love and presence. And these things can lift us to new heights of spiritual joy and victory, even in the face of unanswered prayer or continued suffering.

The apostle Paul suffered a severe physical affliction, a "thorn in the flesh" as he called it, from which he entreated God to deliver him. But after pleading with the Lord three times, he came to the realization that this thorn would remain to pierce and harass him to the end of his days. God gave His apostle the assurance, "My grace is sufficient for you" (2 Cor. 12:9), and Paul submitted to the will of God.

KEEP ON PRAYING

I have a word of advice to you if you are discouraged because of unanswered prayer: Keep on praying. Whether or not God answers your prayers the way you wish He would, it is your privilege and obligation to continue praying. Even though Paul no longer asked the Lord to remove his painful affliction, he never ceased thanking Him for His blessings, requesting His help, and interceding for others. Yes, we must maintain a life of prayer throughout our entire earthly pilgrimage.

Some Christians are puzzled, however, when faced with the question of whether or not to continue praying for some specific matter. They wonder at what point they should simply leave it in God's hands without any further mention. The apostle Paul had to learn that the Lord was not going to remove his "thorn in the flesh." But some of our petitions are of such a nature that it isn't so easy to come to a similar conclusion.

If you have prayed for something over a period of years and nothing has happened, should you continue to pray? Or should you simply commit the matter to the Lord, leave it with Him, and forget it? It all depends on the object of your prayers and the leading of the Holy Spirit. If you are praying, for example, for the salvation of a friend, or asking for spiritual victory in your life or in the life of someone else, you must continue to make these requests as long as you live. You see, some circumstances call for ongoing prayer.

When you are sure your request is unselfish and you know of no reason an affirmative answer could hinder the cause of God, keep on praying. Do so with the assurance that your heavenly Father knows when a yes to your petition will promote the greatest good. Then He certainly will give you the desire of your heart. So again I say, keep on praying!

But there are also occasions when you should *not* keep repeating a certain request. This is sometimes true when you pray for physical healing or for some kind of material benefit. As you sense through the inner voice of the Holy Spirit that it is *not* the Lord's will to give you what you desire, your prayer for a specific situation should be discontinued. Simply leave the matter in God's hands, for He "does all things well."

We received a letter that illustrates beautifully what I'm talking about. It was written by an aged woman whose husband had gone to be with the Lord. Lonely and ill, she was hardly able to care for herself. She mentioned that even though she had asked the Lord to heal her, she concluded that it was not His will to do so. Then she added, "I grow weary of people who call themselves faith healers and act as if we Christians should be spared all physical suffering and illness. Don't they realize that God can teach us things in this way that we can learn in no other? Don't they know that He is preparing us for heaven? I am so glad that I have learned to say, 'Your will be done.' I simply ask for your prayers that I will learn what He wishes to teach me, and that I will have grace to meet each day's trials as they come." This testimony exemplifies real faith.

Christian friend, do not let yourself become discouraged and defeated when your prayers go unanswered. When the petitions of your heart seem to fall on deaf ears, follow the five steps we've talked about. Then you too can find victory and joy even in the face of seemingly unanswered prayer.

SELF-STUDY

1. Name four Bible characters whose prayers were answered.
   a.
   b.
   c.
   d.

2. What five steps should you follow when your prayers are not answered?
   a.
   b.
   c.
   d.
   e.

3. Which phrase below best summarizes the teaching of James 4:3 about unanswered prayer?
   _____ (a) We have asked to make someone else happy.
   _____ (b) We have asked to satisfy our own wants.
   _____ (c) We have asked but don't intend to listen to God's answer.

4. How does an acknowledgment of God's power and wisdom help you when it seems that your prayers are unheard?

Thought Question: What do you do when your prayers aren't being answered? What *should* you do?

7

How Can I Do Better?

ALL WHO BELIEVE in Jesus Christ as their personal Savior are the recipients of many wonderful blessings from God. We have experienced the forgiveness of sin, life eternal is our present possession, and the Holy Spirit dwells within us. We know that God our heavenly Father loves us, watches over us, and cares for us as His very own. And wonder of wonders, we as His children are invited to enter into His presence through the portal of prayer. Think of it! We have the blessed privilege of *talking with God,* and of sharing with Him our burdens and our needs.

But sad to say, the opportunity to have an audience with the Almighty has been greatly neglected. This was true even of New Testament Christians. In the Garden of Gethsemane, the Lord Jesus wanted His disciples to pray, but they fell asleep instead. James told the believers to whom he wrote his epistle, ". . . you do not have because you do not ask" (James 4:2). Failing to talk to the Lord about their needs, they became impoverished.

The same laxness is true today. The great majority of Christians are not availing themselves of this wonderful approach to the very heart of God. They do not take advantage of the invitation to talk with the Lord, to fellowship with Him, and to know the thrill of communion with the Creator and Sustainer of all things. And the tragedy is this: Because we are neglectful or weak in our prayer life, we cannot be truly happy in the Lord or in His service.

In this chapter I would like to answer the question, How can I do better in my praying? Here are three suggestions: (1) Pray according to a schedule; (2) Pray with honesty; (3) Pray continually.

PRAY ON A SCHEDULE

A first step in improving your communication with God is to establish a regular program for praying. It would be impossible for me to overemphasize the importance of having stated times to talk with the Lord. Some people object to this approach, claiming that following a pattern causes prayer to become mechanical. I grant you, this is a possibility. The fact remains, however, that most likely you will not achieve a truly satisfying prayer life unless you do set aside specific times every day for communion with your heavenly Father.

An athlete preparing for a championship event is diligent in his training methods. He must exercise strict self-discipline and determination to get himself into proper condition. If he "worked out" only when he felt like it, he would never be ready. It's that way with prayer too! Our secular interests, our earthly ambitions, our discouragements, and a thousand other factors can put us into such an emotional state that we don't feel like praying. But we must pray anyway, even if we don't want to.

The prophet Daniel is an excellent example of consistent personal prayer. He was entrusted with great responsibility, and tremendous demands must have been made on his time. Yet he faithfully *set aside three special periods every day* for communion with God. And even when his enemies had used their influence to enact a law forbidding all prayer, we are told that Daniel "knelt down on his knees three times that day, and prayed and gave thanks before his God, as was his custom since early days" (Dan. 6:10).

The psalmist David declared, "Evening and morning and at noon I will pray, and cry aloud, and He shall hear my voice" (Ps. 55:17). In fact, he placed special emphasis on the early hours of the day. And in Psalm 5:3 he wrote:

> My voice You shall hear in the morning, O Lord; in the morning I will direct it to You, and I will look up.

A few minutes with God in the morning, as you read His Word and pray before entering the activities of the day, is time well invested. It helps you begin your responsibilities in a spirit of praise, gratitude, and conscious dependence on the Lord. It strengthens you to overcome temptation, to guard your words, to manifest love, and to be cheerful in spite of difficult situations. How much better your days will be when you begin them with God!

It is also important to spend a few moments with the Lord before going to sleep at night. As you reflect on the day, thank Him for His grace in keeping you, confess your failures and sins, intercede for those the Lord has laid on your heart, and ask for strength to do better the next day.

Remember, you and I must talk with the Lord every day, regardless of how busy we are. This discipline is imperative to our spiritual development and effectiveness. There may be times we don't feel like praying—when we're discouraged, at odds with someone, or just bone tired. Fellowship with God is especially needed in such circumstances. When we talk with Him, our spirits are lifted, our anger is dissolved, and our weariness seems to vanish. We rise from our knees refreshed and strengthened.

PRAY HONESTLY

The second absolute requisite for effective prayer is honesty with God. You should tell the Lord exactly what is in your heart. In fact, one of the reasons the saying of prayers becomes mere ritual with so many people is their lack of openness with the Lord. They think they can win points with God if they just use the right words. This often happens in our human relationships, simply because others don't really know us. But listen, friend, you and I can never deceive God. The Scriptures tell us that "all things are naked and open to the eyes of Him [God] to whom we must give account" (Heb. 4:13).

The Old Testament believers were forthright and direct when they talked to God. Moses complained bitterly to the Lord because his demand that Pharaoh allow the Israelites to leave

Egypt had been rejected, and the conditions of their slavery had been made even more intolerable.

> So Moses returned to the Lord and said, "Lord, why have You brought trouble on this people? Why is it You have sent me?
>
> For since I came to Pharaoh to speak in Your name, he has done evil to this people; neither have You delivered Your people at all" (Exod. 5:22–23).

The prophet Habakkuk couldn't understand why God was allowing flagrant sins to go unpunished, so he cried out:

> O Lord, how long shall I cry, and You will not hear? Even cry out to You, "Violence!" and You will not save. Why do You show me iniquity, and cause me to see trouble? For plundering and violence are before me; there is strife, and contention arises (Hab. 1:2–3).

On one occasion Jeremiah felt that God had deceived him, and he expressed his sentiment with absolute honesty.

> O Lord, You induced me, and I was persuaded; You are stronger than I, and have prevailed. I am in derision daily; everyone mocks me (Jer. 20:7).

In each of these cases, God's servants openly expressed their feelings. After all, as human beings just like you and me, they sometimes became discouraged or wondered at God's ways. And they expressed their feelings to the Lord and not to the world. In talking with Him they found relief and victory.

You should follow their example when talking with the Lord. If you're fighting a battle with resentment because the Lord took away a loved one by death, tell Him about it. If you're worried about the prospect of going to the hospital for a major operation, express your fears to God. If you harbor ill feelings toward someone who has wronged you and somehow you can't overcome this sinful attitude, confess your weakness to the Lord. Remember, God can help you far more than any human friend ever could. Besides, He knows exactly how you feel, and He is waiting for you to talk with Him.

Let us therefore come boldly to the throne of grace, that we may obtain mercy and find grace to help in time of need (Heb. 4:16).

The Lord Jesus has experienced everything you and I are going through. Though He did not sin, He "was in all points tempted as we are." He knows and understands, and you can come to Him with full confidence. Open your heart, and tell Him everything. We often say that when people discuss facts, incidents, and opinions, they are not really communicating. It's only when they talk about their feelings that they begin to understand one another. In the same manner, God wants us to lay our thoughts and emotions before Him. Talking with Him will help us, and He will respond to our prayers.

PRAY CONTINUALLY

Not only should we have definite periods of time each day for fellowship with God, and not only should we be completely honest when we speak with Him, but we should also pray continually. The Bible tells us in 1 Thessalonians 5:17, "Pray without ceasing."

"But how can I pray all the time?" you may say. "I've got to have my eyes open when I drive my car. My work demands full concentration. Besides, who can pray at a football game when their team has a first down on the six-yard line? No one, not even a preacher, can be praying all the time."

I can understand that kind of reaction, and I recognize the truth of what you are saying. The fact remains, however, that the Bible tells us to "pray without ceasing," and this command is to be taken seriously by every believer. After all, if it could not be followed, God would not have said it in the first place. Then what does this exhortation really mean? How can we pray without ceasing?

First of all, recognize that even the apostle Paul, who wrote the words, didn't go around with his eyes closed and his hands folded all the time. He wrote letters to the churches. He made tents for a living. He took the time to mix and fellowship with other believers. And I think the great apostle may even have attended some of the sporting events of his day, for he did make several references to them in his epistles. We wonder how he practiced his own admonition to "pray without ceasing."

Prayer is not only an activity but also an attitude. It is possible to pray without closing your eyes, folding your hands, or articulating words. When we drive our automobiles, work at our jobs, or gather with friends for fellowship, we can be conscious of God and direct our thoughts upward to Him.

When you're having a pleasant time, think of God's goodness to you and let gratitude surge up from within your soul. When you are facing a difficult problem and you are in a situation where you just can't take time to verbalize a prayer, think of the Lord and your need of His help. As you consciously turn your mind toward God in this manner, you will continually experience the Lord's nearness. Even in moments of bereavement, loss, or disappointment, a feeling of thanks will rise within your heart, and you will enjoy a peace with God that surpasses all understanding. This is what's involved when you "pray without ceasing."

Victor Hugo was right when he said, "Certain thoughts are prayers. Whatever may be the attitude of the body, the soul can be on its knees." James Montgomery beautifully expressed this same truth when he wrote:

> Prayer is the soul's sincere desire
>   Unuttered or expressed,
> The motion of a hidden fire
>   That trembles in the breast.
> Prayer is the burden of a sigh,
>   The falling of a tear;
> The upward glancing of an eye
>   When none but God is near.

Christian friend, do you desire to be more effective in talking with God? Do you want your communion with Him to be more real? Then begin today to practice these three things: pray on a schedule, pray honestly, and pray continually. Reserve a specific time each day to commune with your heavenly Father. In the morning you will find the joy and love you need to face the people and problems of the day. At night it will be easier to fall asleep with a sense of well-being if you have paused to give

God thanks, to ask His forgiveness, to pray for others, and to ask for strength to do better tomorrow.

When you pray, whether in the morning, through the day, or in the evening, talk to your Father in heaven. Be honest with Him. Use reverent but ordinary language. Don't put on airs. Be yourself. Tell the Lord exactly how you feel. Pour out to Him the doubts that disturb you and the complaints and resentments hindering your Christian life. You'll find great relief, and God will meet your needs.

A PRAYERFUL ATTITUDE

Finally, cultivate an attitude of prayerfulness so that in all of life's experiences, whether sad or glad, the thought of your heavenly Father comes to your mind. Your unexpressed meditations and yearnings are noted by Him, and He considers them a part of your communion with Him.

You may well agree with everything I've said in this chapter. You admit that improvement is needed in this area of your Christian experience. But unless you make a determined effort *right now* to do something about it, none of this will do you any good. You intend to do better eventually, but that special occasion never seems to come. In the meantime, your life is powerless and you lack spiritual joy. You would be ashamed to stand in Christ's presence as you are today.

I urge you therefore to begin at *this moment* to set aside time for fellowship with God. He is waiting to respond to your supplication. He wants you to enter into the greatest privilege of your Christian life—the privilege of communication through prayer. His desire is for you to experience a sense of His presence and peace as never before. And He wants to use you as a means of bringing glory to His name and blessing to others. It's *your move!* Starting right now, talk to God with regularity, with openness of heart, and "without ceasing."

Before you can come to God in meaningful prayer, however, you must first come to Christ for salvation. The Bible tells us that "there is one God and one Mediator between God and men, the Man Christ Jesus, who gave Himself a ransom for all" (1 Tim. 2:5–6). The only way you can fully exercise the privilege of prayer is to come to God through the Lord Jesus Christ. Why not bow your head right now and repeat this prayer of faith: "Lord Jesus, I acknowledge that I could never save myself. But believing that You died on the cross in my place, and that You arose from the dead, I do now receive You as my personal Savior. Save me. Amen."

SELF-STUDY

1. How would you evaluate the way you take advantage of the opportunity and privilege of talking with God?
   _____ (a) Take full advantage.
   _____ (b) Take some advantage.
   _____ (c) Neglect it.

2. What three overall suggestions were given to help us do better at praying?
   a.
   b.
   c.

3. What character in the Old Testament is an example of praying on a schedule?
   _____ (a) Abraham
   _____ (b) Moses
   _____ (c) Daniel

Challenge Question: The psalmist David prayed morning, noon, and night. Why not try it the next few days to see how it affects your life.

4. List three Old Testament people who were honest in their prayers to the Lord.
   a.
   b.
   c.

Thought Question: Are you angry with God about something? Sorry for some sin? Bitter? Will you tell God *specifically* about it?

8

Praise: The Forgotten Aspect of Prayer

KING JEHOSHAPHAT WAS in trouble and he knew it. He didn't have an army, and his country was being invaded by a strong force made up of a three-nation confederation (see 2 Chron. 20:1–30). He had no means of stopping them from marching through his land, storming into Jerusalem, and destroying the city. So he called together leaders from throughout Judah to pray for deliverance.

The king's prayer began with the words, "O Lord God of our fathers, are You not God in heaven, and do You not rule over all the kingdoms of the nations, and in Your hand is there not power and might, so that no one is able to withstand You?" (v. 6). Jehoshaphat then went on to praise the Lord for the way He had delivered His people in the past. Then he asked God to have mercy on them one more time.

Jehoshaphat's prayer points up an aspect of prayer we often neglect: the element of praise. His need was urgent. Defeat and terrible suffering were right before him. Yet the king took the time to give praise to the Lord before he asked for help.

Our prayers are filled with petitions for our needs and intercession on behalf of others. We often remember to thank

God for the gifts we receive from His hand every day. And we are sure to express our gratitude for special answers to our urgent requests. But how often do we praise Him? How often do we lift up His name and exalt Him for who He is? Praise is an important part of the prayers of the Bible, and it ought to be a regular part of our prayers as well.

But we may not be praising the Lord in our prayers because we aren't sure what He expects. We feel that we don't really know how to praise Him in a proper manner. In this chapter we will give some suggestions for praising God in prayer.

FOCUS ON GOD

Perhaps one reason we don't praise the Lord more when we pray is that we don't really have a clear vision of the One to whom we are praying. We are addressing *God* when we pray. Sometimes, in the informality and general disrespect of our age, we lose sight of the fact that we are praying to the Sovereign Lord of heaven and earth.

Notice what the Bible says about those who interceded for Peter when he was in prison. They were conscious of the fact that they were praying to God for his deliverance. "Peter was kept in prison, but constant prayer was offered *to God* for him by the church" (Acts 12:5). Commenting on this verse, R. A. Torrey wrote:

> In order that a prayer should really be unto God, there must be a definite and conscious approach to God when we pray. We must have a definite and vivid realization that God is bending over us and listening as we pray. (*How to Pray,* p. 31.)

Yes, our prayers are to God—the One who is the Sovereign Lord of all. When we are consciously aware that we are addressing the holy, transcendent, personal God, and that He is listening to us, we will want to offer Him praise.

How do we begin to give the Lord the kind of praise He truly deserves? Everything about Him is deserving of more adoration and exaltation than we could ever hope to offer. Dick Eastman, in his powerful little book *The Hour that Changes the World,* wrote, "The possibilities for praise stretch beyond the limits of our imagination. Because God has no limits, our praise is limitless." A study of the Psalms provides us with a model for giving praise to the Lord. We will focus on *what* we should praise God for, *when* we should praise Him, and *where* we should praise Him.

PRAISE GOD FOR WHAT HE IS AND DOES

We can begin by praising the Lord for His characteristics. He is the infinitely holy God. His perfection is absolute. In Him there is no hint, no shadow, of imperfection. Our praise in prayer can therefore center on the excellence of His nature and character, especially as they relate to us and our world. Let's look at the pattern set forth by the writers of the Psalms.

God's Greatness

The psalmists exalted the Lord by praising Him for His greatness. These verses magnify the Lord as ruler:

> Oh, clap your hands, all you peoples! Shout to God with the voice of triumph! For the Lord Most High is awesome; He is a great King over all the earth (Ps. 47:1–2).

David expressed his praise for the Lord's greatness with these words:

> Great is the Lord, and greatly to be praised; and His greatness is unsearchable (145:3).

The greatness of God's works is set forth in this statement by the psalmist:

> Blessed be the Lord God, the God of Israel, who only does wondrous things! (72:18).

The Lord is our great God and king. We cannot measure His greatness, but we can praise Him for it—and for the wonderful things He does for us.

God's Goodness

The writers of Psalms gave praise to the Lord for His goodness. That goodness is made known to us in His mercy, His love, and His grace. Note the admonition in this verse:

> Oh, that men would give thanks to the Lord for His goodness, and for His wonderful works to the children of men! (107:8).

David wrote:

> Because Your lovingkindness is better than life, my lips shall praise You (63:3).

God's Protection

We also praise God for the way He watches over and protects His own. We may have no idea of what He is protecting us from, but we do know that His watchful eye is always on us. Without His protection, where would we be? Let us praise Him for it, as the psalmists did.

> But I will sing of Your power; yes, I will sing aloud of Your mercy in the morning; for You have been my defense and refuge in the day of my trouble. To You, O my Strength, I will sing praises; for God is my defense, the God of my mercy (59:16–17).

These words were written by David when he was hunted by men who were sent by Saul to murder him. God is our Protector.

God's Deliverance

We can praise God too because He is our Deliverer. Not only has He delivered us from our sin through the sacrifice of Christ, but He also helps us in day-by-day living. He has rescued us in Christ, and we can exalt His name for our salvation.

> My mouth shall tell of Your righteousness and Your salvation all the day (71:15).
>
> My lips shall greatly rejoice when I sing to You, and my soul, which You have redeemed (71:23).

These are but a few of the aspects of God's character and work for which the psalmists praised Him. He was also praised for His name (113:1); His mercy and truth (108:4); His glory (148:13); His word (33:2–4); and His justice (101:1). As you read the Psalms, watch for additional aspects of God's nature and works that are worthy of praise when you pray.

WHEN SHOULD WE PRAISE GOD?

The Psalms tell us not only *what* we should praise God for, but when we should praise Him.

In the Morning

A good way to begin the day is to offer praise to the Lord. It gives Him glory as the new day begins. It also gets us ready for whatever may take place throughout the day. It gives us a proper perspective for the ups and downs, temptations and joys, worries and pleasures that the day may bring.

> But I will sing of Your power; yes, I will sing aloud of Your mercy in the morning; for You have been my defense and refuge in the day of my trouble. To You, O my Strength, I will sing praises; for God is my defense, the God of my mercy (Ps. 59:16).

Every Day

Our praise, if modeled after that of the psalmists, will be lifted up to the Lord every day. What a shame it would be if at some time during the course of every day we did not give praise to our God!

> Every day I will bless You, and I will praise Your name forever and ever (145:2).

At All Times

Our praise to the Lord should have no end; it should be continual.

> I will bless the Lord at all times; His praise shall continually be in my mouth (34:1).

Praise to the Lord should always be sounding forth in our hearts. We should continually be offering to Him the "sacrifice of praise" which the author of Hebrews spoke about (13:15).

Forever

The praise to the Lord that begins here on earth will be lifted up to the Lord for all eternity. The psalmist wrote:

> I will praise You, O Lord my God, with all my heart, and I will glorify Your name forevermore (86:12).

When should we praise the Lord? Anytime! No one time is more appropriate than another. But we should, every day, lift up our praise to the God who loves and saves us. "His praise shall continually be in my mouth" (34:1).

WHERE SHOULD WE PRAISE GOD?

The psalmists set no limits on where we should give praise to our Lord. Some of the appropriate places to give God praise are mentioned in the following verses.

In Church

God's name should be praised, of course, when we are assembled with our fellow believers for formal worship. As the worship leader directs us, both in song and in prayer, we will join hearts and voices and sing together: "Praise God from whom all blessings flow." The 150th Psalm begins,

> Praise the Lord! Praise God in His sanctuary; praise Him in His mighty firmament!

In Informal Fellowship

When believers in Christ get together, one of the things they will do naturally is praise the Lord. One of my most memorable prayer times was when I was part of an international group of believers who had never met one another. We began with a time of prayer. As we bowed our heads, the leader asked us to give brief prayers that exalted some aspect of God's character. Some praised Him for His love; others for His goodness. By the time the prayer session was ended, we felt a strong sense of unity and love. The psalmist wrote:

> I will praise You forever, because You have done it; and in the presence of Your saints I will wait on Your name, for it is good (52:9).

Before the Unsaved

Our praise to God does not always have to be among fellow believers. David, fleeing from Saul, sang:

> I will praise You, O Lord, among the peoples; I will sing to You among the nations (57:9).

Sometimes it is good to exalt His name publicly, so that all may hear. In doing this, we give God special honor. We also declare our faith and may become His instruments to bring unsaved people to Him.

A MIGHTY CHORUS OF PRAISE

Praise is a universal and never-ending phenomenon. The hosts of heaven have been praising God from the time they came into being. In Job 38:7 we are told that they "sang together" and "shouted for joy" as they watched God produce the heaven and the earth, and part of that rejoicing was certainly praise. Even in the tribulation, the angels will shout their praise to the Lord. Of Christ they will say:

> Worthy is the Lamb who was slain to receive power and riches and wisdom, and strength and honor and glory and blessing! (Rev. 5:12).

When we lift our hearts in praise to the Lord, we become part of a great chorus of praise that has been offered to the Lord since the beginning of creation and will never end. We join the angels in bringing to the Lord the adoration that He alone deserves.

> Bless the Lord, you His angels, who excel in strength,
> who do His word, heeding the voice of His word.
>
> Bless the Lord, all you His hosts, you ministers of His,
> who do His pleasure (Ps. 103:20–21).

Ours is not a solitary voice when it is lifted in praise to God. It becomes one with a mighty chorus as we magnify the Lord by acclaiming His greatness and the wonder of His works among men.

God is worthy of the praise we offer Him. In fact, if we neglect to do so, we overlook one of the most important and beneficial aspects of our spiritual lives. "Whoever offers praise glorifies Me," the Lord said (Ps. 50:23).

Consider your own life of prayer. Have you forgotten to praise God? If so, begin to give praise to our Sovereign Lord. Praising God may be our duty, but it is also a delight that will fill our lives with His blessing.

SELF-STUDY

1. List three reasons we may not be giving praise to the Lord when we pray.
   a.
   b.
   c.

2. We should praise God for His attributes. We named four of them in this chapter. Name four others, giving Scripture verses to support them.
   a.
   b.
   c.
   d.

3. Mark the following statements about *where* to praise God. *True* or *False.*
   _____ (a) The morning is the best time to praise God.
   _____ (b) Our prayers should always begin and end with praise to the Lord.
   _____ (c) We will praise God forever.
   _____ (d) God doesn't need our praise because the angels in heaven praise him.

4. When should we praise God, according to this chapter?
   a.
   b.
   c.

5. What verses tell us that we are not alone when we offer our praise to the Lord?

9

Prayer: Public and Private

"I'M DISCOURAGED," a Christian confessed, "about my prayer life. I pray, but it seems that nothing happens. When the pastor prays in church, I don't even pay attention anymore. He always says the same thing and I just tune him out. But even my private prayer times seem hollow. I'm sure my prayers must seem stale to God. Besides, He already knows what I'm going to say. What can I do?"

This person is facing a problem many believers have confronted. He needs to realize anew that prayer is not just a religious exercise we go through to conform to some regular ecclesiastical pattern. It is a personal encounter with God. Just as our conversations with people with whom we have an intimate and important relationship are alive and vital, so also can our communion with a holy and loving God be real and fresh.

So let's look at some ways we can keep our prayer life, whether public or private, alive and effective.

PUBLIC PRAYER

We are assembled in the sanctuary or auditorium for our Sunday morning worship service. The minister moves to the platform for the pastoral prayer. We listen in for a little while. We are willing to let him do the praying for us. Before long our minds have wandered. We find ourselves planning the week's activities. We wonder who is sitting with Mrs. Tasma this morning. We calculate how much money we'll have left to purchase new clothes after paying the bills. Or we think about our granddaughter in Florida. Before we know it, the prayer is over—and we have missed an excellent opportunity to join with our fellow believers before the throne of grace. Even more, we have undermined the sense of unity in prayer that the Lord desires and the pastor is assuming he has.

How can we turn the pastoral prayer into a vital part of our own personal prayer activity? Here are some suggestions.

Establish a Right Outlook

Establish the function and purpose of the pastoral prayer. Corporate prayer was an important part of the life of Israel and the early church. God wants His people to come together as one and unite in praise, petition, and intercession. See the pastoral prayer as an opportunity for you to fulfill God's desire for corporate prayer.

Clear Your Mind

When the prayer time comes in the order of worship, concentrate on praying. Push all the cluttered thoughts of a busy life out of your mind and get ready to pray. Keep your attention focused on God during the prayer. If you catch yourself drifting off in your thinking, bring yourself sharply back to the prayer. It will be tough discipline at first, but you will soon find yourself able to stay focused on God during the whole prayer.

Pray with the Pastor

Join him in your mind and heart as he prays. As he gives praise to God, exalt the Lord in your thoughts. When he asks for God's blessing, agree within. While he is praying for those in the congregation with special needs, you pray for them too. If you will unite your thinking with his, you will become part of the corporate prayer.

I'll never forget the first church service I attended in England. When the pastor rose to pray, I heard a strange murmuring sound. I wondered what it was. Then I realized that it was the people's way of joining their pastor in prayer. And in the black churches I've attended, I've heard a chorus of "amens" as the congregation joined the pastor in prayer.

My "amens" are silent. I keep my murmuring to myself. But I've found both of these helpful in keeping corporate prayer alive, fresh, and vital in my life.

If you will follow these principles, you will develop an attitude about public prayer that can make it an important part of your personal prayer life.

PRIVATE PRAYER

Now, what about our private prayers? What can we do to keep our personal times from becoming stale or discouraging? How can we make personal prayer effective and productive—and keep it that way? It will help if we expand our vision of the purpose of private prayer. True, it is a time for praise, thanksgiving, petition, and intercession. These elements have been discussed in other chapters of this book. But if we add to these some new elements, it can bring an exciting new dimension into our prayer experience. Let us therefore consider private prayer as a place to cultivate our relationship with God, to engage in spiritual warfare and bring evangelism into our lives. As we look at each of these in detail, we will see how they can become a means of bringing depth and new life to our prayers.

Prayer and Meditation

We don't need to do all the talking when we pray. Sometimes the best thing we can do is to be quiet. This gives us the opportunity to use our minds to reflect upon the greatness and goodness of God. It gives us a chance to examine our lives—to take a careful and honest assessment of where we are spiritually. And it provides us with a good opportunity to get a better perspective on ourselves and our relationship with the world around us.

Some of us can clear our minds and focus on God the moment we begin to pray. Once in a while, because of the urgency of the moment, we may have to. But most of us need a little time to clear away the clutter and junk so that we can come into the presence of God with a clear and open mind.

This process will not be easy at first. So much is going on in our world. And we do need to talk to the Lord about most of the things we bring with us into the prayer closet. But gradually those things will drift away or be taken care of. We grow inwardly silent. We become ready to talk face-to-face with the One who has called us to prayer.

It's like meeting a good friend we haven't seen for several months. In a flurry of quick conversation we exchange greetings. Then we catch one another up on all the important news. We answer the questions we have for one another. When that is finished, we enter a deeper phase of conversation. We get beyond the informational and down into the emotional and spiritual levels of communication.

It's often like that with God. Once we've gotten the business matters out of the way, it's time to move on to deeper things. We consciously begin to place our lives into His control. We deliberately surrender to Him those things that have become so important to us—our dreams, our ambitions, our reasons for pride, our love for the things of this world.

We turn over to the Lord the things we are concerned about, and the things that are burdening us. In a definite conscious choice of the will, we fulfill what Peter recommended, "Casting all your care upon Him, for He cares for you" (1 Peter 5:7). We relinquish our efforts to protect ourselves and to make things comfortable for ourselves and we give them over to God.

As we quiet ourselves before the Lord, we will also become aware of some sins that need to be confessed. We will repent of the wrong things we are doing. We will agree with God that they are sinful, and we will pledge ourselves to forsake them. As the prayer session continues, the Lord will point out things we are *not* doing. We'll confess those "sins of omission" and promise to try to fulfill the Lord's commands.

As our quietness and surrender to the Lord continues, we

will begin thinking about God Himself. Focusing on His nature and character and on the infinite perfection of His holiness and love, we will worship Him. We will exalt Him, lift Him up, glorify His name. Recognizing that He is far above us, we will see Him as our sovereign Lord, our heavenly Father, our omnipotent God. We will see Him as our Master, Savior, and Friend.

The French theologian Francois Fenelon wrote, "Be silent, and listen to God. Let your heart be in such a state of preparation that His Spirit may impress upon you such virtues as will please Him." The Holy Spirit is our Leader, our Searcher, our Convicter, our Guide. As we rid ourselves of the surface matters of life, grow quiet, and meditate on God, we will find that our private prayer sessions will be enriched and will become more important to us than ever.

Combating the Enemy

Private prayer is also a time for fighting against our spiritual foe. Sometimes our place of prayer needs to be turned into a battleground. We need to use prayer as a strategic weapon against our defeated but still very powerful enemy. There's a real danger of so filling our prayer time with requests and petitions that we leave whole segments of our lives unguarded.

Ours is no ordinary foe. We are not fighting a flesh-and-blood enemy; we are wrestling "against principalities, against powers, against the rulers of the darkness of this age, against spiritual hosts of wickedness in the heavenly places" (Eph. 6:12). We are fighting the devil and his host of demons.

The devil is the ruler of this world. He reigns over those who are not believers and who are still dead in their sins (Eph. 2:1). In fact, we who are saved "once walked according to the course of this world, according to the prince of the power of the air [Satan], the spirit who now works in the sons of disobedience" (2:2). Even though we have moved "from darkness to light" (Acts 26:18), we still must battle with the forces of darkness.

The Bible tells us that Satan is at war with us. He is a fierce foe, a "roaring lion, seeking whom he may devour" (1 Peter 5:8). He is a skilled deceiver, sometimes taking believers captive and having them do his will (2 Tim. 2:22–26). He will even appear as an "angel of light" (2 Cor. 11:14), turning what seems to be good into something wicked and destructive.

Satan has had years and years of experience. He is skilled at using the world and the flesh to tempt us. He discourages us. He disheartens us. He points out every weakness, every flaw, every disappointment.

Nevertheless Satan is still a defeated foe. Paul told us that Jesus Christ disarmed him and his forces, making a public spectacle of them by His sacrifice on the cross (Col. 2:15). And James urged, "Resist the devil and he will flee from you" (4:7). We do that in prayer. We claim the victory of Christ for ourselves. We enlist the Holy Spirit's help in seeing where we are weak and vulnerable. We stand against Satan in prayer, fending him off and causing him to flee.

Our weapons are spiritual: we have the power of God to pull down strongholds (2 Cor. 10:3–5). Only by using the sword of the Spirit, the Word of God, and the resource of prayer can we successfully battle Satan and achieve final victory (Eph. 6:17–18). In this we follow the example of Epaphras, who agonized (wrestled) in prayer for the believers at Colosse (Col. 4:12).

Evangelism

Prayer is also a place for the beginning of our evangelistic effort. It begins with intercession in behalf of those whose lives are in the grasp of Satan. He blinds the minds of unbelievers so that they will not see and receive the truth of the gospel (2 Cor. 4:4).

When we single out an unsaved person for prayer and the witness of the gospel, we are launching an attack on a corner of Satan's kingdom. Prayer is what opens the way so that the gospel will be understood and received.

We want to win our neighbor to Christ. Before we even think about witnessing, we need to bring that neighbor's need before the Lord in prayer. As we pray, we will not only grow in our concern for that person, but we will be led to a good time, place, and strategy for presenting the gospel. Prayer leads to action—soon it won't be enough just to pray. We will want to do something about it.

This is true of the loved ones in our family who are not born again. We want to see our mom and dad, son and daughter come to Christ. We find it difficult to witness to them. We look for opportunities that don't seem to come. Or we have spoken to them about Jesus Christ, and they have rejected Him. They have let us know that they resent it if we talk to them about the Lord.

But we can pray. Regularly, fervently we can ask, seek, and knock. We can move ahead in faith, knowing that the one who blinds the eyes of those who are perishing (2 Cor. 4:4) is not going to have the final say.

What seems impossible to us is easy for the Lord. He can make it happen. Therefore, we need to keep on praying for that unsaved loved one. We should ask God if He wants us to get into the heat of the battle. We can then follow the leading of the Holy Spirit, recognizing that the One who is in us is greater than the one who is in the world (1 John 4:4).

Prayer is personal. It is the intimate, vital communication link between God and us. Public or private, we can make every prayer session relevant and effective. As we add to our prayers the elements of meditation, warfare, and evangelism, we will begin to find our prayer sessions more effective and valuable than ever.

SELF-STUDY

1. Before you begin, list three or four reasons that prayer can become stale and ineffective in the life of a Christian.

2. List the three recommendations given in this chapter for making the pastoral prayer more vital.
   a.
   b.
   c.

3. Mark the following statements about private prayer. *True* or *False*.
   _____ (a) If we aren't talking, we aren't praying.
   _____ (b) It takes time to clear the clutter out of our minds when we begin praying.
   _____ (c) We shouldn't bother God with the surface things in our lives.
   _____ (d) When we meditate in prayer, the Holy Spirit points out our sins to us.

4. How do we confront the enemy in prayer?

5. What does 2 Corinthians 4:4 tell us about Satan that makes evangelistic praying so important?

PRAYER NOTES

PRAYER NOTES

PRAYER NOTES

PRAYER NOTES

PRAYER NOTES

PRAYER NOTES

PRAYER NOTES

PRAYER NOTES

PRAYER NOTES

PRAYER NOTES

PRAYER NOTES